United States Presidents

Herbert Hoover

Paul Joseph
ABDO Publishing Company

visit us at
www.abdopub.com

Published by Abdo Publishing Company, 4940 Viking Drive, Edina, Minnesota 55435.
Copyright © 2001 by Abdo Consulting Group, Inc. International copyrights reserved in all countries. No part of this book may be reproduced in any form without written permission from the publisher.

Printed in the United States.

Photo Credits: A/P Wide World, Corbis

Contributing Editors: Bob Italia and Kate A. Furlong
Book design/maps: Patrick Laurel

Library of Congress Cataloging-in-Publication Data

Joseph, Paul, 1970-
    Herbert Hoover / by Paul Joseph.
       p.   cm. -- (United States presidents)
    Includes index.
    Summary: A biography of Herbert Hoover, thirty-first president of the United States, describing his career as a mining engineer, millionaire businessman, statesman, humanitarian relief worker, and president during the Great Depression.
    ISBN 1-57765-301-7
    1. Hoover, Herbert, 1874-1964--Juvenile literature.
  2. Presidents--United States--Biography--Juvenile literature.
  [1. Hoover, Herbert, 1874-1964. 2. Presidents.] I. Title.
  II. Series: United States presidents (Edina, Minn.)
  E802.J67 1999
  973.91'6'092--dc21
    [b]   98-24021
                                        CIP
                                         AC

Contents

Herbert Hoover

*H*erbert Hoover was not like other politicians. He was not a great speaker or even a lawyer. Instead, Hoover was a scientist and a businessman. He became a politician because he wanted to help others.

Hoover's parents died when he was young. His uncle in Oregon raised him. Hoover went to college and became a successful mining **engineer**. During **World War I**, he led relief efforts in Europe. Then he worked as U.S. Food **Administrator** and Secretary of **Commerce**.

In 1928, Herbert Hoover became the thirty-first American president. When he took office, the U.S. **economy** seemed strong. But in 1929, the economy started to fail.

A long period of hardship fell across America. It became known as the **Great Depression**. Hoover was blamed.

Hoover continued to work hard for America after he left office. In time, he became known for his great contributions to the U.S. and the world.

President Herbert Hoover

Herbert Hoover (1874-1964)
Thirty-first President

BORN:	August 10, 1874
PLACE OF BIRTH:	West Branch, Iowa
ANCESTRY:	German-Swiss, English
FATHER:	Jesse Clark Hoover (1846-1880)
MOTHER:	Hulda Randall Minthorn Hoover (1848-1883)
WIFE:	Lou Henry (1875-1944)
CHILDREN:	Herbert Jr., Allan
EDUCATION:	Local schools, Friends Pacific Academy, Stanford University
RELIGION:	Quaker
OCCUPATION:	Engineer, writer
MILITARY SERVICE:	None
POLITICAL PARTY:	Republican

OFFICES HELD:	Chairman of Commission for Relief in Belgium, U.S. Food Administrator, Chairman of European Economic Council, Secretary of Commerce
AGE AT INAUGURATION:	54
YEARS SERVED:	1929-1933
VICE PRESIDENT:	Charles Curtis
DIED:	October 20, 1964, New York City, age 90
CAUSE OF DEATH:	Internal bleeding

Birthplace of Herbert Hoover

Young Bert

*H*erbert Clark Hoover was born in West Branch, Iowa, on August 10, 1874. Everyone called him Bert. Bert's father, Jesse, worked as a blacksmith. He also sold farm machinery. Bert's mother, Hulda, was a teacher. Bert had a brother, Tad, and a sister, May.

Bert's family belonged to a religious group called the Quakers. They believed in living a simple life, working hard, and helping others. These values stayed with Bert his whole life.

When Bert was six, his father died. Hulda held the family together. She worked as a **seamstress** and a Quaker minister. But Hulda died when Bert was nine. So relatives cared for the Hoover children.

In 1885, Bert moved to Newberg, Oregon. He lived with his uncle, John Minthorn. His uncle was a doctor and a farmer. Bert worked on the farm. He also attended a Quaker school called the Friends Pacific Academy.

When Bert finished school, he and his uncle moved to Salem, Oregon. His uncle started a **real estate** business. Bert worked there as an office clerk. At night, he took business classes.

Bert wanted more education. His uncle hoped Bert would attended a Quaker college. But Bert wished to become an **engineer**. So in 1891, he moved to California. There, he attended a new school called Stanford University.

Tad, Bert (right), and May Hoover

Student & Engineer

*A*t Stanford, Hoover studied **geology**. He also started a successful laundry business, delivered newspapers, and worked for the university. Hoover spent his summers working as an assistant geologist for the U.S. government.

Hoover as a student at Stanford University

Hoover found time to have fun, too. He managed Stanford's baseball and football teams. He was president of the Stanford Geology Club. And he was class **treasurer**.

During his last year at Stanford, Hoover met Lou Henry. She was a geology student, too. Hoover and Lou had much in common. They quickly fell in love.

Hoover graduated from Stanford in 1895. He took a job in a California gold mine. He pushed a mining car and shoveled **ore**. Hoover worked long hours and made little money. But he gained excellent experience.

When the gold mine closed, Hoover took a job with Louis Janin. Janin was a mining **engineer**. At first, Janin hired Hoover as a typist. But he soon sent Hoover on mining jobs in New Mexico, Colorado, and Arizona.

Hoover as a mining engineer in Australia

In 1897, Janin helped Hoover get a job with Bewick, Moreing & Co. of London, England. They sent him to Australia. He taught Australians about America's mining methods. While in Australia, Hoover discovered a rich gold mine. It earned him and the company much money.

World Traveler

*I*n 1898, Charles Moreing offered Hoover a job in China. Hoover accepted. In a **telegram**, Hoover proposed marriage to Lou Henry. They were married in California on February 10, 1899. That same day, they boarded a ship to China.

In China, Hoover acted as the Chief **Engineer** of the Bureau of Mines. He helped the Chinese government find many coal fields and **minerals**.

In 1900, the Hoovers were caught in the Boxer Rebellion. Chinese peasants tried to force all foreigners from China. The Hoovers narrowly escaped harm.

In 1901, Hoover became a junior partner with Bewick, Moreing & Co. The Hoovers moved to London. In 1903, they had a son, Herbert Jr. Five weeks later, Bewick, Moreing & Co. sent the Hoovers on a world journey. Hoover looked for new business for the company. In 1907, their son Allan was born.

By 1908, Hoover was a wealthy man. He formed his own business and engineering company. He started mining projects and helped companies manage their money.

In 1908, Lou Henry Hoover posed with sons Allan (left) and Herbert Jr. in London.

Public Service

*H*oover's new business was a success. But Hoover became bored with making money. He wanted to move into public service.

World War I began in Europe in 1914. Hoover was in London, England, when it happened. The war trapped thousands of Americans in Europe. Hoover organized a relief center. It helped Americans get home safely.

Later that year, a British **blockade** stopped food shipments to Belgium. Hoover headed the **Commission** for Relief in Belgium (CRB). It raised money to feed more than 10 million Belgians.

During World War I, Hoover formed many other relief efforts. They fed and clothed millions of children.

In 1917, Hoover became the U.S. Food **Administrator**. Hoover asked Americans to limit the food they ate. He wanted to be sure America had enough food to send to its troops fighting in Europe.

After **World War I** ended, Hoover directed the American Relief Administration. It fed 350 million people in 21 European countries.

Hoover's efforts in Europe made him famous. He decided to seek the **Republican nomination** for president. Instead, the Republicans chose Warren G. Harding. He became the next president.

A U.S. Food Administration poster urging Americans not to waste food

FOOD WILL WIN THE WAR
You came here seeking Freedom
You must now help to preserve it
WHEAT is needed for the allies
Waste nothing

UNITED STATES FOOD ADMINISTRATION

Secretary of Commerce

*H*oover became Secretary of **Commerce** in 1921. He kept the job for eight years. He worked under Presidents Harding and Coolidge.

Hoover wrote a highway safety code. He improved airline safety. And he encouraged industries to **standardize** their products. This lowered the cost of goods and created new jobs.

In 1921, Hoover planned **irrigation** and power developments along the Colorado River. Two years later, he formed the American Child Health Association. It improved hospitals and helped sick children in need.

Hoover also served as president of the Better Homes organization. It lowered the cost of new homes. This helped more Americans become homeowners.

In 1925, Hoover warned President Coolidge of **economic** trouble ahead. He believed banks were lending money recklessly. This put many Americans into **debt**. And he believed stocks were selling for more than their worth.

But the **economy** seemed healthy. Most Americans had jobs. Many people were making money on the **stock market**. So Coolidge did not act.

In 1927, the Mississippi River flooded. Hoover quickly organized a flood relief program. It fed, clothed, and housed more than 600,000 flood victims.

Hoover's great work made him popular. In 1928, the **Republicans nominated** Hoover to run for president. He ran against **Democrat** Al Smith.

Hoover promised shorter working hours and more **public works** projects. He also promised to help struggling farmers. Voters elected him the thirty-first president of the United States.

A campaign poster of Hoover and Curtis during the 1928 election

For President — HERBERT HOOVER

For Vice President — CHARLES CURTIS

The Making of the Thirty-first United States President

1874

Born August 10 in West Branch, Iowa

1885

Moves to Oregon

1895

Graduates from Stanford University; works in California gold mine

1901

Becomes a partner with Bewick, Moreing & Co.; begins to travel the world

1903

Herbert Jr. born in London, England

1907

Allan born in London, England

1917

Becomes U.S. Food Administrator

1919

Directs American Relief Administration

1921

Becomes Secretary of Commerce

Herbert Hoover

1897
Hired by Bewick, Moreing & Co.; sent to Australia

1899
Marries Lou Henry; sails to China to develop mines

Historic Events during Hoover's Presidency

★ Construction begins on Empire State building in New York City

★ C.W. Tombaugh discovers the planet Pluto

★ Construction begins on Hoover Dam on the Arizona-Nevada border

★ Adolf Hitler appointed German Chancellor

1908
Retires from Bewick, Moreing & Co.; starts his own business

1914
Helps establish World War I relief organizations; begins public service life

1928
Elected president

1929
Stock market crashes

1932
Loses election to Franklin Roosevelt

1964
Dies in New York City on October 20

PRESIDENTIAL YEARS

President Hoover

*P*resident Hoover wanted every American to share in the nation's wealth. He wanted to see a nation "built of homeowners and farm owners." And he wanted to see them all secure.

President Hoover created new organizations to help Americans. The Federal Farm Board aided struggling farmers. The **Veterans** Administration cared for war veterans. The Federal Bureau of Prisons reformed America's prisons.

Hoover pushed **Congress** to create a Department of Education. He proposed tax cuts for the poor. He established more national parks and forests. And he reorganized the Bureau of Indian Affairs to protect Native Americans's rights.

Hoover also proposed a series of dams in Tennessee and California. These projects created new jobs and energy sources.

Hoover asked Congress for tougher banking laws. But Congress ignored Hoover. And banks kept lending money. More and more Americans went into **debt**.

Then, in 1929, disaster struck the U.S. **stock market**. Stock prices crashed. People who borrowed money to buy stocks could not repay their loans. Banks began to suffer.

Even worse, people had less money to spend. Production slowed. Businesses suffered. A **recession** had begun. President Hoover tried to stop it. He asked business leaders not to fire people or cut their wages. And he asked state leaders to create work programs.

But Hoover's plan did not work. The **economy** slowed even more. By 1931, more than 11 million Americans were out of work. Those who had jobs had their wages cut. Banks began to fail. The recession turned into a **depression**. And the economy just kept getting worse.

Americans gather outside the New York Stock Exchange during the 1929 crash

The Seven "Hats" of the U.S. President

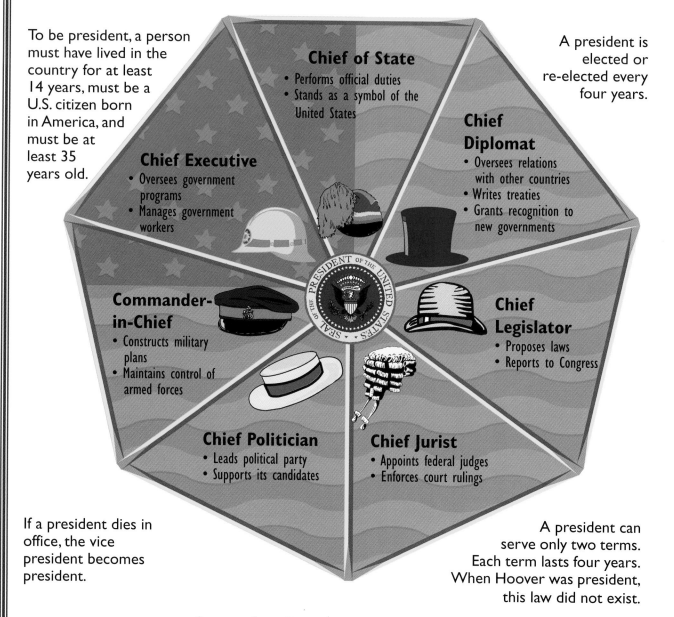

To be president, a person must have lived in the country for at least 14 years, must be a U.S. citizen born in America, and must be at least 35 years old.

A president is elected or re-elected every four years.

Chief of State
- Performs official duties
- Stands as a symbol of the United States

Chief Diplomat
- Oversees relations with other countries
- Writes treaties
- Grants recognition to new governments

Chief Executive
- Oversees government programs
- Manages government workers

Commander-in-Chief
- Constructs military plans
- Maintains control of armed forces

Chief Legislator
- Proposes laws
- Reports to Congress

Chief Politician
- Leads political party
- Supports its candidates

Chief Jurist
- Appoints federal judges
- Enforces court rulings

If a president dies in office, the vice president becomes president.

A president can serve only two terms. Each term lasts four years. When Hoover was president, this law did not exist.

As president, Herbert Hoover had seven jobs.

The Three Branches
of the U.S. Government

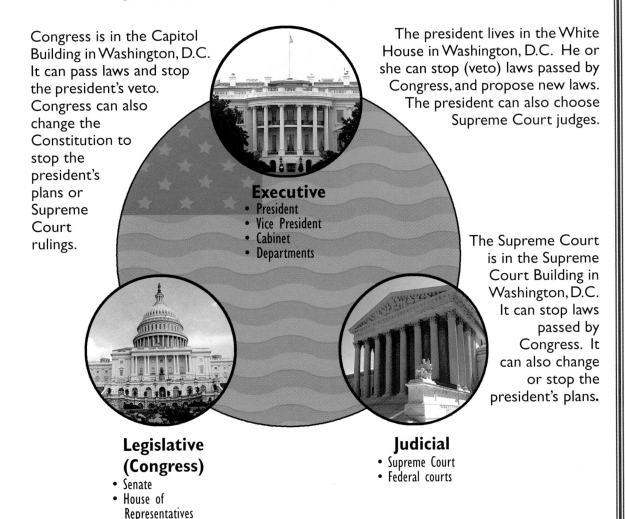

Congress is in the Capitol Building in Washington, D.C. It can pass laws and stop the president's veto. Congress can also change the Constitution to stop the president's plans or Supreme Court rulings.

The president lives in the White House in Washington, D.C. He or she can stop (veto) laws passed by Congress, and propose new laws. The president can also choose Supreme Court judges.

Executive
- President
- Vice President
- Cabinet
- Departments

The Supreme Court is in the Supreme Court Building in Washington, D.C. It can stop laws passed by Congress. It can also change or stop the president's plans.

Legislative (Congress)
- Senate
- House of Representatives

Judicial
- Supreme Court
- Federal courts

The U.S. Constitution formed three government branches. Each branch has power over the others. So no single group or person can control the country. The Constitution calls this "separation of powers."

The Great Depression

*H*oover believed America had to work its way out of the **depression**. He felt that government handouts would hurt America. But he also saw that his plans to fix the **economy** were failing. So in January 1932, Hoover asked **Congress** to pass the Reconstruction Finance Corporation (RFC).

The RFC gave government money to large businesses and banks. Hoover hoped the RFC would help businesses run smoothly again. Then they could give people jobs. But the RFC worked poorly.

During this time, Hoover was up for re-election. He ran against New York's governor, Franklin Roosevelt. But re-election would be difficult.

By now, **shantytowns** called Hoovervilles had sprung up all over the country. They sheltered the homeless. Other homeless people slept under newspapers that they called Hoover blankets. People everywhere waited in long lines for bread. And people marched on Washington, D.C., to demand government relief.

Worst of all, Americans blamed Hoover for starting the **depression**. Roosevelt was easily elected in 1932.

Hoover's last days as president were not easy. He tried to turn the **economy** around. But **Congress** did not agree with Hoover's plans.

Then in February 1933, banks across the nation shut down. Hoover did not have time to fix the problem before Roosevelt took office in March. The depression would not end until **World War II**. Historians call this period the **Great Depression**.

A Hooverville in Seattle, Washington

After the White House

*A*fter leaving the White House, Hoover stayed busy. In 1936, he headed the Boys Club of America. With Hoover's help, 500 new clubs were started. They helped boys who lived on the streets.

World War II began in Europe in 1939 when Germany attacked Poland. Hoover led the Polish Relief **Commission**. It fed thousands of Polish children.

World War II ended in 1945. It had destroyed Europe. Hoover led the Famine Emergency Commission. It fed millions of Europeans while they rebuilt their cities and farms.

In 1947 and 1953, Hoover led special government groups. They suggested ways to cut wasteful government spending. They had great success. **Congress** passed nearly all their suggestions. These groups later became known as the Hoover Commissions.

Hoover spent the rest of his days writing, giving speeches, and advising American presidents. By then, America once again respected and praised him for his hard work.

By 1963, Hoover had grown ill. He refused to give up his work. But his health grew worse. On October 20, 1964, Hoover died from a large **hemorrhage** in his stomach and intestine. He is buried near his childhood home in West Branch, Iowa.

Though he was known as a great problem solver, Herbert Hoover had a difficult presidency. Americans blamed him for the **depression**. But the problems that caused the depression were firmly in place when he took office. Not even Hoover's leadership skills could overcome them.

Hoover meets with poor Polish children shortly after World War II

Fast Facts

- Herbert Hoover was the first president born west of the Mississippi.

- Construction on the Hoover Dam began in 1931. When finished in 1936, it was the largest dam in the world.

- President Herbert Hoover never accepted his salary as president and spent his own money to entertain guests.

- In 1932, President Hoover signed an act making "The Star-Spangled Banner" the national anthem.

- Hoover loved the outdoors. He especially liked to go fishing. He even wrote a book about it, called *Fishing for Fun.*

The Hoover Dam

Glossary

administrator - a person who manages an operation, department, or office.

blockade - when an army shuts off an area to prevent supplies or troops from going into or out of it.

commerce - the buying or selling of goods on a large scale.

commission - a group of people chosen to perform certain duties.

Congress - the lawmaking body of the U.S. It is made up of the Senate and the House of Representatives. It meets in Washington, D.C.

debt - something that is owed to another.

Democrat - a person who is liberal and believes in a large government.

depression - a period of time when there is little buying and selling, and people are out of work.

economy - the way a state or nation uses its money, goods, and natural resources.

engineer - a person who plans buildings, machines, roads, bridges, and canals.

geology - the science of Earth and its structure. A person who studies geology is called a geologist.

Great Depression - a period of economic hardship that started in 1929 and ended at the beginning of World War II.

hemorrhage - heavy bleeding.

irrigate - to supply land with water by using channels, streams, and pipes.

mineral - a natural element, such as gold or silver, that is not of plant or animal origin.

nominate - to name a person as a candidate for office.

ore - a rock that has enough minerals in it to make it worth much money.

public works - projects paid for by the government, such as roads, dams, or sewers.

real estate - land and the buildings, trees, and water that are on it.

recession - a time when business activity slows. It is not as bad as a depression.

Republican - a person who is conservative and believes in a small government.

seamstress - a woman whose work is sewing.

shantytown - an area of small, poorly-built homes.

standardize - to make everything the same.

stock market - a place where stocks and bonds, which represent parts of businesses, are bought and sold.

telegram - a message sent by coded electrical impulses.

treasurer - a person who takes care of the money for a business or club.

veteran - a person who has served in the armed forces.

World War I - 1914 to 1918, fought in Europe. The United States, Great Britain, France, Russia, and their allies were on one side. Germany, Austria-Hungary, and their allies were on the other side. The war began when Archduke Ferdinand of Austria was assassinated. America joined the war in 1917 because Germany began attacking ships that weren't involved in the war.

World War II - 1939 to 1945, fought in Europe, Asia, and Africa. The United States, France, Great Britain, the Soviet Union, and their allies were on one side. Germany, Italy, Japan, and their allies were on the other side. The war began when Germany invaded Poland. America entered the war in 1941 after Japan bombed Pearl Harbor, Hawaii.

Internet Sites

The Presidents of the United States of America
http://www.whitehouse.gov/WH/glimpse/presidents/html/presidents.html
Part of the White House Web site.

Herbert Hoover Presidential Library and Museum
http://hoover.nara.gov/index.html

These sites are subject to change. Go to your favorite search engine and type in "United States Presidents" for more sites.

Index